Dutch Heart of Man

by
Bob Glaudini

SAMUEL FRENCH

FOUNDED 1830

New York Hollywood London Toronto
SAMUELFRENCH.COM

Copyright © 2007 by Bob Glaudini

IMPORTANT BILLING AND CREDIT REQUIREMENTS

All producers of *DUTCH HEART OF MAN must* give credit to the Author of the Play in all programs distributed in connection with performances of the Play, and in all instances in which the title of the Play appears for the purposes of advertising, publicizing or otherwise exploiting the Play and /or a production. The name of the Author *must* appear on a separate line on which no other name appears, immediately following the title and *must* appear in size of type not less than fifty percent of the size of the title type.

DUTCH HEART OF MAN was presented by Labyrinth Theater Company at the Shiva Theater in the Joseph Papp Public Theater in New York City. The production was directed by Charles Goforth with sets by Narelle Sissons; costumes by Mimi O'Donnell; lighting by Jason Kantrowitz; sound by Elizabeth Rhodes; the production stage manager was Jana Llynn and the stage manager was Richard A. Hodge with the following cast:

FLORENCE . . . . Maggie Bofill
MOMMA and MARTY'S MOM . . . . Maggie Burke
MARTY . . . . David Deblinger
PHYLLIS . . . . Wilemina Olivia Garcia
CUSTOMER NO. 2, BANANAS and CHEF . . . . . . Scott Hudson
DUTCH . . . . Salvatore Inzerillo
CUSTOMER NO. 1 and MRS. STAMEN . . . . Portia

CHARACTERS

Dutch, a terrazzo grinder

Marty, a terrazzo grinder

Florence, cashier, waitress

Bananas, a hod carrier

Phyllis, truck driver

Momma, Florence's mother

Mrs. Stamen, a religious woman

Mom, Marty's mother

Customer 1

Customer 2

Some parts can be doubled: Momma/Mom;
Bananas/Chef/Customer 2; Mrs. Stamen/ Customer 1

SET

A construction site; which transforms to indicate: a gas station,
restaurant, bar, apartment.

Scene 1

(Scaffolding rises up the rough exterior corner section of a mammoth construction project underway. In distance, but a part of the project, and depicted in trompe l'oeil, a nearly-completed cathedral with two blue mosaic, gold-ribbed domes.

Downstage is a 4' x 8', grey plywood tool box, top opened. Chained to it are two large terrazzo floor grinders. Heavy power cords are wrapped and hung on the handles. Dampened sound of construction work from inside the site.

BANANAS, a hod carrier with a heavy hod of wet plaster on his shoulder, makes his way up and across the scaffold. The sound of construction inside the site stops and the sound of men arguing builds quickly. BANANAS, back to audience, pauses on his way across the scaffold to listen. Heated voices stop, and slowly the sound of construction continues. BANANAS moves on until he crosses out of sight.

DUTCH, around 34 years old, comes from the building under construction in an agitated state. He carries a heavy, silver, terrazzo hand grinder. DUTCH, big, rawboned, wears yellow rubber slickers and heavy rubber boots. There's a simple quality to DUTCH, a friendly face, naively earnest, and an obsessive commitment to work.)

DUTCH. *(To himself.)* I don't know, maybe, but it don't have to be like that. I don't think. My opinion.

(DUTCH takes a new carborundum grinding wheel from the toolbox and starts replacing the worn out one on his machine.

MARTY, handsome Italian-Irish, traces of east coast accent, average height but muscular build, thirty-five, also in yellow slickers and boots, pushes a wheelbarrow of watery pucciorino, a waste product of terrazzo grinding, and dumps it into a slag heap circle dammed by sand and crusty slag build up. MARTY is cocky, opinionated, an authority on women.

MARTY goes to the water hose and rinses his hands.)

DUTCH. *(CONT'D)* You believe those guys? They wanted to kill each other.

MARTY. They tape fucking sheet rock. What do you expect from morons? Fucking let 'em.

(MARTY takes a thermos of coffee from the tool box. He pours a cup and lights a cigarette.)

MARTY. *(CONT'D)* Light and sweet. You wanna cup? Italian roast. The best. Help yourself.

DUTCH. What was it with them, something over some politician, or something?

MARTY. The sex thing they're arguing over, like there's a choice in the matter?

DUTCH. That was it, you think?

MARTY. What do I know? But sex will make you do what

you say you're not gonna do, is all I'm saying from my experience. So who's to say right from wrong?

DUTCH. The little guy was saying something about if it was his daughter? I don't think he has one. I may be wrong, but I don't think so. You see him with that rock hammer? That's why I grabbed him like that.

(DUTCH resumes changing the grinding wheel on his machine.)

MARTY. Fuck em. What about tomorrow? You gonna work? I don't know if I wanna Saturday.

DUTCH. I wanna get the base cove in the bathrooms. Get them over with. Sunday, too, maybe, I'll come in to get 'em done.

MARTY. We can knock one off, Saturday, OK, maybe, but I'm not working Sunday.

DUTCH. It'll be quiet.

MARTY. Saturday's quiet enough for me, I want quiet. *(Pause)* I can't believe you're gonna work Sunday.

DUTCH. It's money.

MARTY. You don't buy nothing.

DUTCH. Nothing else to do.

MARTY. How much you got hid under the mattress?

DUTCH. Nothing.

MARTY. I'll bet you do. Tucked under there.

DUTCH. Naw.

MARTY. You got to put the top of the mattress to work, y'know. My mattress could talk, it'd say get up and gimme a rest. *(Beat)* Get something going up there, you won't be working Sundays. You'll be working on top of the mattress grinding on something nice, all your money hid underneath the action, instead of working and grinding fucking terrazzo on Sunday! That's the difference the world's all about, right there. *(Looks for a response, but doesn't see it. Pause.)* You find someone special, some nice girl, is all I'm saying.

DUTCH. You don't have no one, though, I mean, so...I mean, no one special, right? So...y'know?

MARTY. No one special, no, right, on a permanent basis. But we're different in that sense, right? You want someone... I don't know...Special. Permanent. Something steady, right? Ain't that what I hear from you?

DUTCH. Maybe. Yeah, I guess.

MARTY. OK. That's what I'm saying. *(Beat)* You got someone I don't know about?

DUTCH. No. *(Pause)* I did see someone, though, I wanna...though, y'know...

MARTY. What? *(Waits for response.)* Who is this? Who we talking about?

DUTCH. This girl works at Arco. I'd like to get to know her better.

MARTY. She got some nice ones?

DUTCH. What?

MARTY. Some nice ones, y'know, up front?

DUTCH. Come on.

MARTY. What? It's a crime having them?

DUTCH. No.

MARTY. You talk to her yet?

DUTCH. I get gas there now, you know, so, I will. She seems nice. She's friendly.

MARTY. You want a friendly girl, OK, they're around, but, you know, for me, she's got to have some development, if she's

got some, y'know, a set of nice developed size ones, well, any-way, being honest, it's the first thing I check out. *(Beat)* Well...
back at it.

(MARTY rinses the thermos cup and returns thermos to tool box. He goes back inside the building.)

DUTCH. *(Talks to himself.)* I don't think so, though, that you're right about it. Just so you know, I don't think I agree. Not that many. Not that are friendly. Not really.

(DUTCH finishes changing the six-inch grinding wheel. There's the whine of MARTY'S grinding machine starting up. Sounds of construction grows in rhythm. Sound of traffic noise, the deep bass of sound systems, horns, car alarms join the construction sounds until the car sounds, and traf-fic noise takes over.)

Scene 2

(Arco gas station. FLORENCE is behind the counter. She's in her well-lived thirties. Her often friendly, spirited person-ality has worn down some. PHYLLIS, 35, solid build, and possessing a confident attitude, wheels in a dolly load of beer.)

PHYLLIS. Hey, Florence, how's it going?
FLORENCE. You believe they asked me to cover the next shift?
PHYLLIS. So you say no, right?
FLORENCE. They know I work the other job.

PHYLLIS. So you say no.
FLORENCE. It's like it doesn't fucking register.
PHYLLIS. So you said no?
FLORENCE. What?
PHYLLIS. You said no to them.
FLORENCE. Sure, I told 'em no.
PHYLLIS. Let me park these.

(PHYLLIS moves on to the rear. DUTCH ENTERS.)

FLORENCE. *(To DUTCH.)* What can I do you outta?
DUTCH. Some gas, but I think, maybe, I'll just get some beer first, or some soda, maybe.

(DUTCH crosses up to disappear in the rear. Customer 1 enters and gives FLORENCE a credit card.)

CUSTOMER 1. I want to fill it on six.
FLORENCE. Six?
CUSTOMER 1. Yeah, six. I want to fill it.

(PHYLLIS comes from the back with the empty dolly. Gives FLORENCE paper work. DUTCH returns with a six-pack of Sprite.)

FLORENCE. As it is I rush home to clean myself up, check on Momma, and worry I make the other job on time. I'm only here three years. I'm there seven.
PHYLLIS. The restaurant's on Orange, right?
FLORENCE. Yeah, on the corner of Fuller and Orange. Edward's Cafe.

PHYLLIS. I've been meaning to get by there. The food's good?

FLORENCE. *(To CUSTOMER 1.)* Declined.

CUSTOMER 1. It can't be. Try it again.

(FLORENCE runs the card again.)

FLORENCE. *(To PHYLLIS.)* People love the baby backs. The chili burgers. Most things are pretty good. People love the shakes. We put an egg in and a little real vanilla extract. *(To Customer.)* It's declined. It happens.

CUSTOMER 1. I'm gonna run out of gas. I got my kids in the car.

FLORENCE. You want to try ten?

CUSTOMER 1. Yeah. Sorry.

FLORENCE. No problem.

(CUSTOMER 2 ENTERS. He gets behind DUTCH, and waits with increasing impatience.)

CUSTOMER 1. Thanks.

PHYLLIS. I could eat some ribs right now

FLORENCE. Come by sometime, I'll fix you up. *(To CUS-TOMER 1.)* Declined.

CUSTOMER 1. Ten dollars? It's declined?

FLORENCE. I'm sorry.

CUSTOMER 1. Can you try five?

(FLORENCE runs the card.)

FLORENCE. *(To PHYLLIS.)* We still have to go out and have fun like we said. *(To customer.)* Says declined.

CUSTOMER 1. Oh, man, oh. *(Beat)* Damn! *(Beat)* You can't do three dollars can you, because I'm gonna run out with my kids?

FLORENCE. I'm not allowed to do under ten.

(PHYLLIS heads out.)

PHYLLIS. I'll see ya, Florence.

FLORENCE. I'm gonna call you.

PHYLLIS. Alright.

(Phyllis exits.)

CUSTOMER 1. You did five.

FLORENCE. I know I did five. I shouldn't have. I can't do three. I'll catch all kinds of hell.

CUSTOMER 1. I got kids in the car. See the Buick? I got four kids in the car.

FLORENCE. I can't do three.

CUSTOMER 1. It don't make sense. You did five. It don't make sense you don't try three.

FLORENCE. Okay.

(Runs the card.)

CUSTOMER 1. I wouldn't be begging but...

FLORENCE. It says keep the card.

CUSTOMER 1. Keep the card?

FLORENCE. *(Hands it back to her.)* You can have it. I don't want it. I'm telling you, is all, it says keep the card.

(The CUSTOMER is at a loss as to what to do.)

CUSTOMER 2. Can we move on?

DUTCH. I'll do the five. You don't mind. I'll get the five?

CUSTOMER 1. This is embarrassing. Gimme your number. You help me out, I'll get it back to you. I got my kids and I got to get to San Pedro.

DUTCH. It's okay. I'll take care of the five, it's OK with you.

CUSTOMER 1. This is embarrassing. Yeah. OK. Because I'm in a situation.

FLORENCE. Five on pump six.

CUSTOMER 1. If you can make it nine-fifty, I can get a pack of cigarettes. You gimme your address though, I'll send it to you tomorrow.

DUTCH. Naw, forget it, give her smokes. Pass it on sometime.

CUSTOMER 1. *(To FLORENCE.)* Camel filters in a box.

FLORENCE. Five on pump six and a box of Camel filters.

CUSTOMER 1. *(To DUTCH.)* I do the same thing. I see someone in need. Same thing. I have it, I give it.

DUTCH. Alright. Take care. Don't worry. It's no big deal. Pass it on.

CUSTOMER 1. I always pay my way. I don't like to beg. Thanks, though. I'm gonna do that, too. I'm gonna pass it on.

(CUSTOMER 1 EXITS.)

DUTCH. Fill it on one.

FLORENCE. You're the Good Samaritan from the bible?

DUTCH. No, not really.

FLORENCE. *(As she runs the card.)* I'll do the nine-fifty on six. Plus a six of Sprite and fill it on pump one.

DUTCH. I know it's tough sometimes. I understand that, y'know. A lot of people out of work. A lot of people have it tough. It's not easy. I couldn't help hear you work two jobs. So I understand, someone's down a little on their luck. I don't mind, y'know, helping out.

CUSTOMER 2. Look, I'm waiting here.

DUTCH. You would've told me you were in a hurry, you could've cut in, gone ahead.

(FLORENCE hands him the card back.)

FLORENCE. Thank you.

(CUSTOMER 2 steps around DUTCH.)

CUSTOMER 2. Four quarts of fifty weight.

DUTCH. Thanks. I'm Dutch, by the way.

FLORENCE. Okay, Dutch.

DUTCH. Okay. Next time. Florence, right?

CUSTOMER 2. *(Under his breath.)* Jesus, holy shit.

DUTCH. What? You say something?

CUSTOMER 2. Not to you, I didn't.

FLORENCE. Fifty weight?

CUSTOMER 2. Yeah. Four quarts of fifty weight.

(DUTCH EXITS the Arco mini-mart and waits outside. Inside, CUSTOMER 2 takes the oil from FLORENCE, and EXITS the mini-mart. Outside the mini mart, DUTCH approaches CUSTOMER 2.)

DUTCH. Pardon me, but you don't have to be rude.

CUSTOMER 2. What are you saying?

DUTCH. You see I'm talking to the young lady.

CUSTOMER 2. You got some problem?

DUTCH. I don't think I have a problem. I don't know. Maybe I said something. I don't think I did, but maybe I said something that offended you. Maybe that's why you give me looks, you gotta say something rude. I didn't mean to be rude to you, but if I did, I want to say I'm sorry, because I think we have to do what we can, you know, not to cause problems, and be patient, y'know, to make life easier.

CUSTOMER 2. You for fucking real?

DUTCH. I thought maybe you swore at me under your breath because I said something that got taken the wrong way.

CUSTOMER 2. You want a problem, you got a problem, 'cause you sound like you want one.

DUTCH. I know how to have a problem. I don't want a problem, that's the point, you're not listening to me.

CUSTOMER 2. I'm listening to your ass. I'm tired of listening. I'm tired of people wasting my time, standing in line talking about nothing, when I want to pay my money and get on my way.

DUTCH. I understand that.

CUSTOMER 2. I got to put oil in my car and hope it don't run right out so my engine don't burn up before I make it to my job and you want me to stand around while you talk to some woman. Get her phone number! Talk to her on your own damn time! Not when I'm late for work! You want to get down to the elastic don't make me wait and listen to your tired ass trying to get a leg over because you don't know what to say anyway.

DUTCH. I'm not trying to get no leg over. Maybe I just

want to get to know her. What's wrong with that? That's no reason for someone to be rude.

CUSTOMER 2. You ain't nothing to me, and I don't care how nice you want to be, or what you got to say about anything. Where you think you're at? Look around, this is a gas station. See, the sign says Arco!

(CUSTOMER 2 EXITS.)

DUTCH. *(Calling after him.)* I know it's a gas station. *(Adamantly; as though in a private conversation.)* These are places we meet. We make contact here. You can be patient, y'know, make life easier in these places. Even in gas stations, even at an Arco, and everywhere! *(Calling after Customer 2.)* Everywhere! Even in line in the store! I have had conversations with people! Right there in line in a supermarket! Good conversations! You may not agree, you have a right not to, but that's what I think! Because that's what's happened! *(To himself.)* What are we anyway? We animals or something? We can talk to each other if we want. And if I want to meet her. If I want to say something nice. I can do that. I can say something nice, if I want. *(Louder, yells off.)* We're human beings last time I looked!

(Construction sounds grow loud, overwhelming the sound of cars and traffic.)

Scene 3

(Construction site. MARTY, bare-chested, yellow overall slickers peeled down to waist, is washing off at a hose. High pitch sound of grinder from inside the site shuts off.

BANANAS, the hod carrier, crosses the scaffold with a heavy hod of wet plaster on his shoulders. DUTCH wheels a wheelbarrow of the watery pucciorino out of the building and dumps it into waste pond. He looks up at the hod carrier crossing out of sight.)

DUTCH. Imagine called Bananas.
MARTY. What?
DUTCH. The hod carrier.
MARTY. What about him?
DUTCH. They call him Bananas.
MARTY. It's his name.
DUTCH. You think so?

(DUTCH strips his yellow slickers down to his waist, pulls off his shirt, and washes off at the hose. MARTY takes a large lunch cooler from the tool box.)

MARTY. He carries fucking plaster up and down a scaffold like a monkey. What do you expect? *(Sits)* I finish sealing the room, I'm done today, I'm taking off. I go out tonight I don't want to feel like I still got the machine in my hands. You know what I mean? I'm going to find something soft with some big soft things up top. You know, big enough I can see the top part moving where they swell up. That's what gets my attention. You know, how it moves there, a little sway type motion when they walk. You've seen it. The top part here. Not the whole thing. I don't mean nothing crude, y'know, not jiggling, or bouncing.
DUTCH. Oh, yeah, I know.
MARTY. Not that.
DUTCH. No. I know.

MARTY. It's more a subtle thing for me. *(Gestures to indicate it.)* This part up here that trembles and rolls a little when she moves. You see it in the supermarket when they're coming down the aisle toward you. The part right here has a motion, a rolling motion. That's what I'm gonna find tonight, a soft, rolling, gentle rocking motion.

(MARTY opens his large lunch cooler. DUTCH goes to the tool box and takes out a regular sized lunch box. MARTY busies himself looking at the food in the cooler. Checking what's what.)

DUTCH. I'm staying till I knock off the rest of the cove, and cut the corners. There's a quarter inch of cement before you see the chip. Thicker in some places, half inch, and hard. What were they thinking they poured it? Then let it set-up a month before we get on it. They think it isn't cement or something, doesn't keep getting harder? And those big rose number two chips are hard. I went through four number six wheels and I'm only half done. I had to put my leg to the wall to bare down to get anywhere. I don't want to come back to it tomorrow.
MARTY. So, you're not working tomorrow?
DUTCH. Yeah, I'm working.
MARTY. No, but you said —
DUTCH. That's what I'm saying. I want to finish the cove today, so I can do the entrance way tomorrow, so Monday we can move to the big room, and be on the floor. Give my arms a break. Let the floor machine do the work.
MARTY. They paid overtime I might be tempted to work Sundays.
DUTCH. *(Defensively)* They're behind.

MARTY. They want you to work a hundred hours a week. They even paid time and a half it'd be another matter. Cheap fucks. You want some of this? I got plenty. My mom puts in extra.

DUTCH. I'm okay.

MARTY. *(Checking sandwiches.)* They don't want you out having too much fun, if you knew the truth. You have too much fun out fucking the ladies, you don't give a shit so much about working all the time. That's why I know you don't get laid like you should, you wanna work seven days a week. *(Sizes up all the food.)* Take something. I got three sandwiches. I got sausage, I got salami, I got eggplant and onions. I got some kind of pasta-fungoo-alu-you-too with olives, mushrooms, and sweet peppers. I got provolone, mortadella. Look, I got homemade cookies.

DUTCH. Your mother made all that?

MARTY. What'd you bring?

DUTCH. Baloney sandwich, I think —

MARTY. Oh, fuck that —

DUTCH. — or turkey ham —

MARTY. — fuck turkey ham —

DUTCH. — I can't tell —

MARTY. Fuck, don't eat that. She gives be stuff lasts me a week. Not just the lunch, y'know, but manicotti, lasagne, a roast chicken. She's a regular fucking supermom. *(Beat)* Where's your mother live? Dutch, you're mother? She live here?

DUTCH. She's dead.

MARTY. Dead. *(Beat)* Damn. *(Beat)* That's the worst. Jesus, I couldn't handle that. I don't want my mom ever to die. *(Beat)* I'd probably fucking starve for one thing.

DUTCH. I don't eat that much anyway. I mean, not like

you, I guess. You get good food.

MARTY. You know what? I'm gonna have the sausage. You want the salami or the eggplant?

DUTCH. Maybe the salami. *(Takes it.)* You sure its OK? I'm not big on eggplant. I never heard of an eggplant sandwich.

(They start eating the sandwiches.)

MARTY. Eggplant and onion. Olive oil. You gotta like eggplant to like it though.

DUTCH. I don't think I like it that much. Your mother must like to cook. She makes a lunch for you like this, like it's a meal. My mother never cooked. She didn't know how. She burned everything.

MARTY. My mother would shoot herself she burned something. She would shoot herself in the head in the kitchen. Shoot herself and bleed to death on the floor.

DUTCH. Well, my mother hated to cook so she let it burn, I think. She made beans, that was about it. They always burned.

MARTY. She burned beans?

DUTCH. And I remember the stew, too. She tried once, anyway, to make it, and it burned all up.

MARTY. Oh, man, no. That's fucking awful.

DUTCH. The only other thing she made was rice she burned.

MARTY. She burned rice?

DUTCH. It was always burned. I got used to it, but I don't eat any rice now. You could make it perfect, it tastes burned to me.

MARTY. Not my mom's.

DUTCH. It would taste burned to me.
MARTY. My mom's wouldn't taste burned. Never.
DUTCH. I can't help it. That's how it tastes to me.
MARTY. My mom doesn't burn nothing.

(BANANAS appears upstage with the now empty hod and makes his way down the scaffold.)

DUTCH. No, I know your mom's a great cook. I'm saying my mom was lousy, a lousy cook. No, look at this food, your mom knows what she's doing. Everything's perfect. It's my mom burned everything. She hated to cook. I don't hold it against her. It was just something, it was just one of the things she hated to do.
MARTY. You said the house burned down, didn't you? She burned down a house, or something, your mom.
DUTCH. Something with the oven.
MARTY. Some house you lived in?
DUTCH. She forgot, I think. She said, fuck it, good riddance. She was tough, what I remember. I was a kid.

(BANANAS puts his hod aside and rinses off at the water hose before lighting a smoke.)

MARTY. Don't let the thing with your mom stop you with women for the rest of your life.
DUTCH. I like women.
MARTY. Uh-huh. You talk to the Arco woman yet?
DUTCH. It was busy there, so I'm going by this other place she works.
MARTY. She works two jobs?

DUTCH. You know the Edward's on Orange? It has good baby backs?

MARTY. I'm gonna stop by, you know, and see.

MARTY. See what?

DUTCH. If she likes me. If there's something.

MARTY. I could go by, sometime, start a conversation, let her know she's the lucky one to meet you. It'd be in a round-about-way. Nothing obvious. It's nothing for me to talk to women, y'know? Let me know, y'know, if you want me to, no problem. *(Folds the wrapping around his sandwich.)* OK. You know what? I'm not even gonna finish this right now. I'm gonna seal the room and get the F out of here. You want anything, help yourself. Try the cookies.

(MARTY goes to the tool box and pulls out a five gallon can of sealer, gloves, rags, and a squeegee. He goes inside.)

DUTCH. *(Talks to himself.)* I'm not so sure I'd want you to go by and talk to her for me, though. I'd rather you didn't actually. No, just don't. You hear me? Just don't go and do it.

(Eats. Watches BANANAS smoke.)

DUTCH. You eat lunch? Hey, Bananas. Bananas. You eat? I got some extra.

BANANAS. Cigarette.

DUTCH. Yeah, but you gonna eat? *(Gestures; unsure BA-NANAS understands English.)* Eat?

BANANAS. Cigarette.

DUTCH. No, I know, but you want to eat? *(Pause)* I'm only asking, because I got some extra. I got a sandwich. Extra.

You wanna eat something? Marty brought lunch so... a lot of food his mother made. She makes him food. Italian type. If you want this — it's extra food. It's not Italian. Baloney, I think, or turkey-ham, some mayonnaise on it, too, though. It's better'n from the lunch truck, if you're waiting for it. Take it. No problem. You should eat. I mean, if you want it.

BANANAS. OK. Thanks.

(BANANAS takes the sandwich. Eats.)

DUTCH. I called you Bananas because I heard them call you that but I don't know if it's your name.

BANANAS. Bananas...

DUTCH. Yeah? Is it your name?

BANANAS. They call me Bananas. The boss.

DUTCH. Yeah, I know. *(Beat)* I'm Dutch.

BANANAS. Dutch?

DUTCH. They call me Dutch since I was little. I don't mind, though. I don't know if it's the same with you to be called Bananas. If you don't mind, or not. I don't know.

(BANANAS grows suspicious, puffs up and becomes a little macho.)

BANANAS. You making fun?

DUTCH. What?

BANANAS. *(Steps forward.)* Making fun of me.

(DUTCH RISES, smiling, hands up in surrender to placate the misunderstanding.)

DUTCH. Hold on.

BANANAS. What? This is funny?

DUTCH. *(Patiently)* I called you Bananas because I heard them call you Bananas, and maybe I shouldn't have, y'know, if you don't like to be called it.

BANANAS. The boss calls me Bananas.

DUTCH. Yeah, that's what I heard, but if you don't like it, he shouldn't call you Bananas. He's the boss, I understand, but if you don't want to be called a name like Bananas you don't have to. You can tell him. He's probably a good man. Probably he'll understand. You carry a hundred pounds of mud on your shoulder, up and down all day long for him, so you can tell him, y'know, provided you want to, you can say to him I'd rather not be called Bananas.

BANANAS. Bananas my name.

DUTCH. OK, OK, I hear you.

BANANAS. He asked me where I'm from. Where my family from, my dad, you know. I said, off the banana boat, boss. So... I made a joke...so he calls me Bananas.

DUTCH. Well, if you say it's your name. If that's what he calls you, he kind of gave you that name, but if that's it now, and you don't mind that's it, you don't mind Bananas, then, that's it. You can be called what you want, that's what makes this country great.

BANANAS. USA.

DUTCH. Yeah, yeah. USA.

(BANANAS has finished eating the sandwich.)

BANANAS. This is good. This baloney.

DUTCH. There's another sandwich here, if you want. Ital-

ian sandwich. Eggplant.
BANANAS. Eggplant?
DUTCH. And onions. Olive oil.

(BANANAS takes the eggplant sandwich.)

BANANAS. Eggplant. *(Smells it.)* Mmmmm. OK. *(Rolls it back up in wrapping.)* Later. I'm gonna eat it.
DUTCH. Maybe some cookies? Homemade. Chocolate chip. Here, have a cookie.

(BANANAS takes a cookie.)

BANANAS. Coffee?
DUTCH. Well, sure. Here. Cookies and coffee, why not?
BANANAS. Good chocolate chip.
DUTCH. I don't eat a big lunch. I eat a big breakfast.

(BANANAS drinks the coffee down.)

BANANAS. Gotta work.
DUTCH. You don't take much of a lunch break.
BANANAS. Eat and work.
DUTCH. OK.
BANANAS. I like work. Thanks. Eat later.
DUTCH. I like to work, too, that's why I'm here like you on a Saturday, but a man's entitled to a lunch break. If you don't want to take it that's one thing.
BANANAS. Thanks. Good food. Eat and work together.

(BANANAS hoists the hod and moves off stage right.)

DUTCH. *(As BANANAS EXITS)* I like to work too, but you have certain rights, inalienable rights. That's all I'm saying. I'll work seven days a week, but I know my rights. I understand a man likes to work. He has to, and he wants to.

(DUTCH pulls the top of his yellow overall slickers back up. Puts on yellow slicker jacket. Puts on large rubber boots. Puts on goggles. Puts on a waterproof yellow hat.)

DUTCH. *(Talks to himself.)* I think I can go by and talk to her without you and do all right. It's nice of you to offer but I think I'd rather you kept out of it. Kept all the way out.

(Puts on nose and mouth air-filter mask. Puts on large black rubber gloves. Hoists a large coil of heavy electrical cord around one shoulder and a large coil of water hose around the other. Picks up a big silver handheld grinder machine and walks into the building.)

Scene 4

(Edward's Coffee Shop. Night. FLORENCE wears a waitress uniform that reveals cleavage. She places new orders at kitchen window while loading up on plates of ready orders. She rings order bell in process. The CHEF APPEARS, an apparition in white, partially seen in steamy, smoky hot light.)

FLORENCE. Waiting on a breast on white no tomato working.

(FLORENCE EXITS.)

CHEF. No one's on vacation here. Sixteen hours. No help. Hell hot kitchen.

(FLORENCE RETURNS pushing a trolly of dirty dishes.)

FLORENCE. Bus the tables. Scrape and scald the dishes. Ugly chicken feet hands.

(FLORENCE EXITS with dirty dishes. CHEF places orders on kitchen window counter, rings order bell.)

CHEF. Ten years stinking grease no room no air.

(FLORENCE RETURNS picks up waiting order.)

FLORENCE. Spicy backs twice. Fries, fries. Salad, soup.

(FLORENCE EXITS with the order.)

CHEF. Grease flair burned hair. Bum wrist. Potato elbow —

(FLORENCE RETURNS with trolly of dirty dishes.)

FLORENCE. Asshole comment table one. Grab ass table two. Stiffed tip table three.

(FLORENCE EXITS with dirty dishes. CHEF places orders on kitchen counter, rings order bell.)

CHEF. Baby backs double mash burger drowned crispy fries.

(FLORENCE RETURNS, picks up order.)

FLORENCE. Naked burger, one time. Chile fries. Super baby once. Breast on white double tomato.

(FLORENCE EXITS with order.)

CHEF. Under paid under the table bad back no insurance lousy sleep up at four too tired angry wife no sex —

(FLORENCE rushes by with trolley of dirty dishes. CHEF puts an order on the counter and rings the bell.)

CHEF. Breast on white no tomato looking good ready and waiting your eyes only!

(FLORENCE flies by to snatch up the breast on white.)

FLORENCE. Here I come. GOTTA LOVE YA!

(She EXITS with the order. Lights fade in restaurant. Neon Edwards sign on outside. DUTCH stands on sidewalk looking nervous and forlorn but trying to get it together to go in.)

DUTCH. *(Nervous, quick tempo.)* Oh, boy. Oh, boy. OK. OK. OK. Oh, boy. Alright, alright, now. OK. OK. Just go in, go on in. No problem. Simple thing. Go on in.

(Looks as though he might, but gets cold feet. Pats his hair in place.)

DUTCH. Say, how are you? Nice to see you. Nice day? Met you at the Arco. Filled it up on pump one. There was a man in there had it kind of rough. Another fella was kind of rude. Had a little talk with him. You probably don't remember me. My name is Dutch. I don't know if you would want to, but we might go out sometime. Well, that'd be anywhere you want to go, anywhere at all. *(Pats hair, adjusts shirt.)* Oh, boy. Oh, boy. OK. OK. OK. Oh, boy. Alright, alright, now.

(FLORENCE APPEARS inside the restaurant and starts shutting off lights.)

DUTCH. It may be too late. There's a right and wrong time. Maybe this isn't too good. Late as it is now. *(Pats hair takes a breath.)* She's a friendly person, though. A good person. I'm gonna go in. Just go in and act casual. Say how it's a funny thing, a coincidence type of deal. *(Beat)* I'm Dutch. The Arco? I work in terrazzo. I'm a terrazzo grinder. A terrazzo man. Terrazzo worker. Terrazzo is a cement and marble deal. Floors. Showers. Bathrooms —

(The CHEF comes out of the restaurant, EXITS.)

DUTCH. Oh. Looks like they're closing up. Maybe it's

not a good time. Maybe she's got someone anyway. Probably.
Probably has. I don't know. Yeah, closing. Late, I guess. Too
late now.

(FLORENCE finishes her closing routine.)

DUTCH. Oh-oh, this is her. This is her coming. OK. OK,
then. Say Hello, yep, Dutch, from the Arco?

(FLORENCE steps out of the restaurant.)

DUTCH. Well, I guess you're closed.
FLORENCE. Yeah, ten. Sorry.
DUTCH. Yep, well, some other time.

(He starts to back away.)

FLORENCE. You're the good Samaritan that bought the
guy gas.
DUTCH. You remember me?
FLORENCE. You're name's Dutch, right?
DUTCH. I didn't know, all the people you meet, to say
anything. "Florence." I remember you is what I mean. This is
a pretty good coincidence. I heard about your ribs, and thought
I'd give them a try.
FLORENCE. I'm sorry.
DUTCH. That's OK.
FLORENCE. They'll be here tomorrow. Four to eight rib
special.
DUTCH. I was driving by I saw the place. OK, then, nice
to see you again. *(Starts off, stops, returns.)* You don't need a

ride, do you?

FLORENCE. No, I have a car.

DUTCH. You're sure, because it's no problem, if you don't?

FLORENCE. I'm sure.

DUTCH. Then you're OK. That's good then.

FLORENCE. It's nice of you to offer.

DUTCH. I can walk you, if you like.

FLORENCE. It's only a couple blocks.

DUTCH. I don't want to intrude. If you want to walk alone, I mean, I understand.

FLORENCE. You can walk me if you want to. I don't want to put you out.

DUTCH. No, I think I'd like it. I don't want to see you walk alone at night.

FLORENCE. OK.

(They walk.)

DUTCH. To be honest, you're doing me the favor because I don't meet many people. I work a lot. I don't have two jobs but I have one long one. I work in terrazzo.

FLORENCE. I don't think I know what that is.

DUTCH. There's tile and there's marble and then there's terrazzo. It's used for floors mainly, sometimes it's used for walls, in bathrooms for instance. For the wainscoating, the wall up to, say, yeah high. *(Indicates chest level.)* You've probably walked on it a lot and didn't know it. It's in some of the fashion malls and a lot of buildings. The colorful floors you see, sometimes that have square or diamond patterns with different colored backgrounds, and the chips of marble showing. That's terrazzo. It doesn't look like much more than plain cement until it's ground down and polished. That's what I do. I'm a terrazzo grinder.

FLORENCE. I'm gonna keep my eyes open for it. *(Pointing the way.)* Down this way.

(They walk on.)

FLORENCE. It's good to have a trained skill. There's probably always going to be things to build has floors to walk on.

DUTCH. Well, I watched you at the Arco. You do your job. I couldn't handle it.

FLORENCE. I know pump one from pump two but it's not a real skill.

DUTCH. You have people skills.

FLORENCE. I can usually spot an asshole. But I don't meet a lot of people to know, really.

DUTCH. Me neither. I do have a friend, a guy I work with, Marty. I know Marty pretty good. I work with Marty. He's a good man, I think, so I know good people are out there. I'm pretty sure you're a good person. It's the way I try and look at people, anyway. I'm thirty four. I'm lucky you remembered me, though, all the people you see, let's say, and I got to talk to you some. Maybe if I come by, say to buy some gas, or come by to try the baby backs, it'd be OK to say hello.

FLORENCE. Come by anytime you want, but we close at ten. The grill's off at nine. I don't remember everyone I meet for the first time. It was so nice what you did, helping that guy out. You stuck with me. I'm in the lot right there. Well, nice seeing you again, Dutch.

DUTCH. You, too. I'm gonna say hello. You'll see me.

FLORENCE. I've a friend, maybe she and your guy from work could meet us or something. She's a girl delivers the beer to the Arco.

DUTCH. I could ask him. Marty likes to have fun. I know the ladies go for him. He's always going out. He knows quite a bit about it. He's good looking. They like him.

FLORENCE. Well, let's talk about it next time.

(FLORENCE EXITS.)

DUTCH. Well, let my nerves settle back down to a normal level. *(Feels heart.)* God, I'm pounding nonstop. Remember to breathe next time. Keep thinking to breathe all the time I'm talking, tell myself, that's right, that's good you're talking, now breathe. Say it quietly in my head, breathe, breathe, breathe... *(Breathes deeply, hands on his rib cage.)* Anything could go wrong at anytime before I see her next time. All this inside me, working away. *(Feels stomach.)* This stomach constantly shifting, doing something, working day and night. The lungs working all the time. Working when I'm sleeping. They could just quit, all the air disappear, and flatten out. All the organs in there. The heart working twenty-four hours a day. It could just squeeze itself closed and stop. The miles of tunnels and pipes, working, pumping, moving things, working, in a relay of things, nerves and things working all the time. Boy. Oh, boy. I sure need to remember to breathe, though, to breathe, that I know.

(HE EXITS.)

Scene 5

*(Construction site. MARTY ENTERS from the building drag-
ging two long lengths of thick water hose. He dumps one
and plays the other one out in order to roll it up. It coils
and kinks up along the ground. He starts coiling it in circles on the ground in front of him, twisting the kinks out,
putting his foot on the coils as he does. The hose gives him
a bad time by refusing to twist into shape.)*

MARTY. This fucking thing.

*(MARTY gives the hose a violent shake in an attempt to get it to
cooperate. DUTCH ENTERS with two long, thick, electrical cables coiled around his shoulders and a hand machine
and a bucket of assorted tools of the trade. He puts them
in the tool box.)*

DUTCH. You got that?
MARTY. This fucking thing.
DUTCH. Hold on.
MARTY. I hate this shit.
DUTCH. Hold up.

*(DUTCH takes up the end of the hose, so it stretches between
them.)*

MARTY. We should have a fucking helper to do this crap.
DUTCH. Twist it the other way.
MARTY. We have to scoop the fucking pucciorino-
DUTCH. No, the right —

MARTY. — change the fucking stones, wash the fucking tools, wind the fucking cords, and this fucking thing.

DUTCH. You're going left. The other way.

MARTY. All the fucking things they invent they don't invent a fucking hose that doesn't fucking act like a fucking idiot.

DUTCH. The other way. The right.

MARTY. What?

DUTCH. The right, you're going left.

MARTY. I'm going right.

DUTCH. The other way.

MARTY. They got smart bombs but they don't got smart rubber that fucking cooperates. No offense but I can't stand this stupid fucking grinding stupid shit work. I'm a fucking tile setter for fuck sake.

DUTCH. Tile's slow, right now.

MARTY. Don't I fucking know it.

(They finally manage to get the things coiled up and they put them in the tool box, and close and lock the lid.)

DUTCH. What was that again? The meat I ate?

MARTY. Veal?

DUTCH. Veal?

MARTY. Yeah, veal.

DUTCH. Veal and what was it?

MARTY. Parmigiana. It's called veal parmigiana.

DUTCH. Oh, yeah, with the cheese. That was good. Real good. Homemade. Thank mom for me.

MARTY. What?

DUTCH. Your mom, you thank her for me.

MARTY. Yeah, OK, I'll tell her, y'know, she's feeding the work force. She'll like that.

DUTCH. Well. Because I appreciate it. *(Beat)* So what do you think?

MARTY. What?

DUTCH. About Saturday.

MARTY. About that, huh?

DUTCH. Saturday night.

MARTY. I know.

DUTCH. I'm going by there for ribs. That's why I'm leaving early.

MARTY. Saturday? The sight unseen thing?

DUTCH. You thought about it?

MARTY. About going sight unseen?

DUTCH. Maybe Saturday night?

MARTY. A charity mission?

DUTCH. I'm going by, so I should know, y'know, if you're gonna do it or not, so if it works out, she can tell her friend that delivers beer.

MARTY. If I don't find something better maybe I'll help you out. If it's casual, and say we meet up, say I come by, see if she's my type or not. She's not my type — she could be, you never know. But, if she's not, why waste my time, right? If she's not what I like in a woman, y'know, with that flow I mentioned? *(Indicates breast area.)* And something here too? *(Indicates butt area.)* I like something going on back there, some fucking meat, y'know. I love the sight. Love it. Nothing like a good derriere, in my opinion. *(Pause)* The truth is I've done anal. I won't lie. They don't all go for it, but you'd be surprised how many they'll try it once, at least. You have to use the right lubrication, and lot's of it, lots of lube, and you have to be gentle but firm. *(Beat)* You never did anal?

DUTCH. What?

MARTY. Anal?

DUTCH. Anal?

MARTY. Anal sex? *(Beat)* I asked have you done it. *(Beat)* Gone anal?

DUTCH. Whoa...

MARTY. I know, it's a crazy thing to do. I'm an animal. The thing is, you tell them they'll enjoy it, that it feels weird, maybe at first, but then, they'll enjoy it, if they relax, that it'll feel better and better, and you GO SLOW. Right? *(Looks at DUTCH, who is perplexed, and reads it as impressed.)* I teach you half the things you know about women, don't I? More than half, in truth, probably, right, since we been working together? *(Beat)* About anal, though, you have to make sure of the timing, because I got a surprise once — talk about pucciorino. Didn't turn me off it, a little embarrassing. I don't know what she ate, Chinese, Mexican, something anyway. Could've been meat and potatoes, anything, by the time it passes through you, right? It isn't everything, anal. It's not the last word, but it's something to try, if you've done everything else. But some of them will start to do it, say, Oh, OK, I want to try it, then go, Oh, no. They change their minds. They'll do that. But others, no problem, they go all the way. They all say it's the first time, though, if they're nice enough girls, y'know, not just doing it for the money, though I've never paid for that, anal, specifically, but my experience is they say it's the first time, and it could be true. You can't really tell with women. But, yeah, I like a good healthy ass with some nice legs, and I like a good set of lips. The face, in general, I like. It don't have to be perfect but — who's to say what's perfect? An OK face, though, in general.

It's gotta be OK, and they gotta be clean, goes without saying, so when I go down south, if I go down south, I'm not gagging. But the personality is important too, I've told you that — so if she's a dog to me, the one delivers beer, I say hello, stay for a drink, y'know, to be sociable, and then move on so my night's not ruined. So, yeah, I can do that for you. If it's casual like that.

DUTCH. So...I'll say, you'll like to meet her friend then?

MARTY. That's what I'm saying. You want me to do that. You want me to. I can meet this Florence you're hot about, too, be objective, if you want my opinion on her.

DUTCH. So I'll tell her Saturday's, OK, if she says she wants to, and this girl delivers the beer wants to?

MARTY. Saturday's my best night, but, yeah, I'll meet her, take a look, like I say.

DUTCH. So, I'm gonna tell her, and hope, y'know, she says yes.

MARTY. Why wouldn't she? You say you told her about me?

DUTCH. Yeah. That you like to go out.

MARTY. You said the women like me?

DUTCH. I told her they did. I told her you were a good looking guy.

MARTY. There it is, then. Nothing but net. *(Beat.)* OK, fuck this, I'm getting out of here. I'll see you in the morning. You let me know.

(MARTY EXITS. DUTCH watches him walk off. Broods.)

DUTCH. Anal? I don't know about you. I think I better say thanks but no thanks, and sayonara to you on the idea, if that's how you're gonna be. *(Darkly)* I could fuck you up. I let it out, I could fuck you up bad. *(Pause)* OK. That's better then, that's more friendly. Glad to hear it. I don't want to have to teach no grown man manners.

(DUTCH EXITS.)

Scene 6

(FLORENCE'S apartment. An iron lung type of contraption is upstage. MOMMA is in it. There's the sound of assisted, or troubled, breathing. A smaller oxygen tank on rollers stands near the lung. FLORENCE ENTERS in a skirt and bra.)

FLORENCE. Do you have to pee? Momma? I don't want to get all dressed up, then you ask me to carry you? *(Pause)* Momma? *(Pause)* You have to go to the little ladies room?

(Pause. Noticeable breathing change.)

MOMMA. No.
FLORENCE. You sure? Because you're gonna have to use the bed pan, if you gotta go, once I get all dressed up. *(Beat)* Momma, you sure?

(Pause. Noticeable breathing change.)

MOMMA. I don't have to.
FLORENCE. You heard me about the bed pan though? *(Pause)* OK. *(Sits to put on her pumps.)* The lady you like from

church is gonna be here. The lady that sings hymns and reads.

MOMMA. Who?

FLORENCE. Mrs. Stamen. The lady from your church.

MOMMA. I don't know her.

FLORENCE. Momma! The one whose husband was killed when the elevator fell. She used to talk about all that trouble he had with his mouth. He was coming from the dentist.

MOMMA. Gawd...

FLORENCE. I asked for her because I know you like her.

(Pause. Noticeable breathing change.)

MOMMA. Not really.

FLORENCE. Come on, you know you like her.

(Pause.)

MOMMA. No.

FLORENCE. Well, I do what I can!

(FLORENCE EXITS to the rear.)

MOMMA. Florence...

(Sound of rhythmical breathing. Stops.)

MOMMA. Florence...My highball.

(Sound of rhythmical breathing. Stops.)

MOMMA Florence...*(Louder, more impatience.)* I want

my highball now.

FLORENCE. *(OFF)* I'm getting the G.D. thing!

(Sound of rhythmical breathing. FLORENCE RETURNS. She carries a tall highball glass.)

FLORENCE. I'm wearing that good perfume I got. You smell it? Estee Lauder.

(She waves her wrist over the iron lung. MOMMA makes a wheezing sound.)

MOMMA. Too strong.
FLORENCE. Don't get like this just because I have some-one coming over. Don't be jealous. I know you. I know how you like men. I remember. After YOU-KNOW-WHO left.

(Labored breathing.)

MOMMA. I didn't run around!
FLORENCE. You want your highball, you'd better be nice.
MOMMA. Gimme my highball.
FLORENCE. You be nice then.
MOMMA. I want my highball!

(She puts a glass straw in the glass and lowers it into the lung so MOMMA can drink.)

FLORENCE. *(As she removes the oxygen feed from MOM-*

MA'S nose.) Let's take this off for a while. You want your oxygen you tell me. But let's take it off so you can have your refreshment. He said he wanted to pay his respects. So we'll stay until the woman from the church comes. We're gonna meet his friend from work, and the gal I've mentioned, Phyllis, delivers the beer to Arco. You do like your highball, don't you? Let's come up for air for awhile. *(Sets the highball aside.)* I'll do your hair. *(Fetches necessary items.)* Put on a little lipstick. Make you pretty.

    MOMMA. Don't fuss...

    FLORENCE. I know you like it.

(She reaches into the iron lung to brush MOMMA'S hair.)

    MOMMA. I hope...he has a job...at least.

    FLORENCE. You heard of terrazzo, mama?

    MOMMA. What?

    FLORENCE. The company he works for does terrazzo.

    MOMMA. What?

    FLORENCE. Terrazzo.

    MOMMA. Never heard of it.

    FLORENCE. It's like a cement with pretty pieces of shiny marble showing. You walk on it all your life and never know it, really, until it's pointed out. I see it all the time now. Let's put a little lipstick on you now. OK, Momma? A little lipstick. Give you a little color, maybe a little blush, too, give your face a little color. This is a pretty rose color. Not too flirty. I don't want you taking him away. He's working on a big school being built near downtown. I think he said it's a Catholic law school. There's a big church on it, a big cathedral looks about done, but the whole thing will take a few years, so he's got plenty of work. Anyway,

he's a terrazzo grinder. He makes it shiny. *(Finishing up.)* Don't
you look nice?

MOMMA. Hope he likes you.

FLORENCE. He likes me or he wouldn't be coming to see
me.

MOMMA. You're not getting younger.

FLORENCE. Don't I know it after all day on my feet.

MOMMA. You need a man.

FLORENCE. OK, Momma.

MOMMA. Try and act like a lady.

FLORENCE. OK, Momma.

MOMMA. He could be a good catch.

FLORENCE. Let's take your support hose off and put your
feet up. We want to remember to put the diaper on.

(She reaches in to pull the stockings off.)

MOMMA. Don't have sex tonight.

FLORENCE. What if I'm swept off my feet?

MOMMA. They get what they want. They don't come
back. They're dogs.

FLORENCE. They're not all dogs.

MOMMA. You run around too much.

FLORENCE. I work two jobs last time I counted. *(Having
removed the support hose.)* There you go.

MOMMA. I won't always be here to give you advice.

FLORENCE. You're not going anywhere just yet.

MOMMA. I might as well.

FLORENCE. You get like this when you're tired. Let's put
your feet up.

(She places a support pillow in the end of the lung and reaches in to put MOMMA'S feet up on it.)

MOMMA. I'm alone.
FLORENCE. Who's here talking to you?
MOMMA. You leave me alone.

(She rubs lotion on MOMMA'S legs and feet.)

FLORENCE. The church is sending someone over. The woman you like. I'm here my lunch break at Arco. I'm here my break at Edward's waiting on you.

MOMMA. I'm lonely. I can't sleep at night. I think of everything. For hours. Everything I've done. The things I've done wrong.

FLORENCE. You get like this, there's nothing I can do. I always have someone with you, don't I? Thank God for your church and that little pension you get. Thank God for social security, and the little medicare left.

MOMMA. I don't want to meet him.

FLORENCE. You're just gonna have to put on your party personality. He wanted to meet you, so I said come a little earlier. I want you to be nice. I know you can. I saw you do it once. *(FLORENCE EXITS rear.)*

MOMMA. You make mistakes in men. *(Pause)* Hear me? *(Pause)* You make mistakes in men. *(Pause)* Florence. *(Pause)* Florence...

(FLORENCE ENTERS adjusting the low cut blouse she has put on.)

FLORENCE. What, mama?
MOMMA. You make mistakes in men.
FLORENCE. I made one, alright.

(Pause. Sound of cackle from MOMMA, takes breath loudly, cackles again.)

FLORENCE. To think what I went through over that idiot. *(Laughs with MOMMA; after it stops.)* One big mistake. *(Beat)* Bottoms up.

(FLORENCE holds the highball for MOMMA to drink. MOMMA slurps up the last of it. Doorbell.)

FLORENCE. That must be my gentleman caller. *(Removes empty glass.)* Be nice you might get another one.

(She EXITS to answer the door.)

MOMMA. Oh, yeah, be nice. Easy for you to say. Easy to say. *(Struggles more upright.)* You're not helpless. *(Pause)* Blind. *(Pause)* Diapers...*(Pause)* On a machine all night to breathe. *(Pause)* Can't smoke! I can't even smoke! *(Pause)* Easy for you to say! *(Pause)* YOU KNOW HOW I LOVE TO SMOKE. *(Beat)* Oh. Oh. Florence? Oh. My chest. Air. Florence. Oh! Oh!

(Pause. A loud burp.)

MOMMA. *(Satisfied.)* Ah! That's better.

(FLORENCE ENTERS with DUTCH.)

FLORENCE. Well, this is my place. Not much but...

DUTCH. No. Looks good. I like the area.

FLORENCE. Would you like a beer or a highball?

DUTCH. What are you having?

FLORENCE. I'm having a highball, but you can have a beer if you want.

DUTCH. No, a highball sounds good, y'know, a special occasion.

FLORENCE. Momma this is Dutch I told you about. *(Motions to DUTCH.)* You have to come here, so she can see you. She sees shapes, anyway.

DUTCH. How are you? How you doing today?

FLORENCE. We're gonna have a highball, Momma. I thought you might want to join us, might want to say a nice Hello, and have one with us.

MOMMA. Hello.

FLORENCE. *(Pointedly)* You do want a highball, don't you, Momma? You're gonna join us, aren't you?

MOMMA. Yes.

FLORENCE. Three highballs coming up.

(She EXITS.)

DUTCH. I admire you. I know it's not easy for you. Florence tells me you're a fighter, though. She said your mind is as sharp as a tack. *(Pause)* Well, I'm in terrazzo work, it's a construction trade, a form of that, of construction. Well, that's what I do, the work I'm in. It's called terrazzo. I'm a terrazzo grinder.

(FLORENCE ENTERS with a drink for DUTCH, which she gives him.)

FLORENCE. Here you are.
DUTCH. Thank you.
FLORENCE. Momma. You being nice? I'm not getting your highball unless Dutch says you're being nice. Is she being nice?
DUTCH. Yes, sure, very nice.
MOMMA. I want a highball.
FLORENCE. I'm gonna get it now, Momma. Company first. I don't think she really understands what terrazzo is.

(FLORENCE EXITS.)

DUTCH. *(Takes a deep breath.)* Well...terrazzo. It's cement with a lot of marble chips in it. You can color the cement, just about any color you want, then they mix in the pieces of marble. They mix it into the cement in a cement mixer and the helpers wheel it in wheelbarrows to men that spread it on the floor. Well, it looks pretty much like cement when it's hard, until we grind it down with machines — that's what a terrazzo grinder does — grinds it down until the marble chip shows, grinds until its smooth and shiny, and you put the sealer on it to bring out the different colors. That's when it's terrazzo.

(FLORENCE ENTERS with MOMMA'S highball.)

FLORENCE. Here you are, Momma.

(She picks up her drink on her way to hold MOMMA'S highball down into the lung so MOMMA can drink from the straw.)

FLORENCE. *(To DUTCH, a toast.)* Here's looking at you?

(DUTCH moves to touch glasses with her.)

DUTCH. Here's looking at you.
FLORENCE. Here's looking at you, Momma.

(They drink.)

DUTCH. Why don't you sit down. You wait on people all day. Why don't you take a rest and enjoy your drink?
FLORENCE. Well...
DUTCH. Let me hold that for you if Momma don't mind. You sit down and enjoy your drink.
FLORENCE. Well...
DUTCH. Go ahead. I can hold it.

(She sits and enjoys her drink. Adjusts her blouse. Looks at DUTCH flirtatiously.)

FLORENCE. Very thoughtful, Dutch.
DUTCH. It's good to just sit down, isn't it? One of the luxuries, to take a break, especially when you work hard.
FLORENCE. You know about the terrazzo now, Momma? Did Dutch explain it? You know what I was talking about now?

MOMMA. No.

DUTCH. You could've seen terrazzo in public buildings, court houses, bathrooms.

MOMMA. No.

DUTCH. In banks, with all the colors of marble in the patterns on the floor and the walls.

MOMMA. No.

DUTCH. Some of the fancy shopping malls.

MOMMA. I never saw it!

FLORENCE. *(Impatiently)* You've seen it. You don't know it until it's pointed out! *(Pause)* You've been in terrazzo a long time, Dutch?

DUTCH. I've been with them about twenty years now.

FLORENCE. Mamma, you hear that? She was at Consolidated Assembly for thirty five years.

DUTCH. That's major.

FLORENCE. She gets a little pension.

DUTCH. That's nice.

FLORENCE. My work, I won't get anything like a pension. There's a turkey at Christmas you can count on.

DUTCH. Well, I get good pay, lot of hours, straight time all the way, but the company isn't making all that much, I don't think. They've been alright to me, I guess. *(Pause)* But it was rough, at first, when I was a kid, a rough haul. I unloaded the boxcars. The marble chips come in burlaps sacks, these hundred pound sacks, and they come in these boxcars. I was fifteen and I thought I'd die. Those bags were up to the ceiling, and the marble dust was bad, and so fine it comes through your handkerchief. You could hardly breathe. It gets all over you, this powder, marble powder. I carried these bags off the boxcar and onto a truck and then unloaded them at the yard. My skin

came off my hands. The burlap wore it right off. They wrapped 'em up with gauze, but it didn't do no good, and they was always there, the owners, Angelo and Pete, when the truck came in, to see if I'd quit. I was skinny then, and had a hell of a time, but I got stronger. I was a helper, then they made me a grinder. Grinding makes your arms strong that's for sure. *(Holds out his arm.)* Specially doing the walls, y'know, holding the machine up all day. I don't have muscles like a muscle man, but they did get stronger.
FLORENCE. Oh, yeah. *(Moves to DUTCH.)* They look good and strong. *(Feels his arm.)* I like a man with strong arms. Oh, my, hard as cement.

(Loud slurping from MOMMA. DUTCH raises MOMMA'S highball glass.)

DUTCH. Looks like we're done here.

(FLORENCE takes the glass from him.)

DUTCH. It's wet work, y'know, the grinding is done wet, all the rough grinding, so the water sprays from the machine. Makes a mess, a sloppy mess they call pucciorino, Italian word, doesn't mean anything. Maybe means slop. Probably does. *(Beat)* When you fine grind you grind dry and there's lots of dust, that fine dust I mentioned, so you can't see as well sometimes.
FLORENCE. I'll bet you're good at it, a good worker.
MOMMA. Florence, I got to go!
FLORENCE. *(Annoyed)* God, I knew it.
DUTCH. What?

MOMMA. I got to go.

FLORENCE. I'm not going to carry you.

MOMMA. I need to make a trip!

FLORENCE. I'm not going to carry you.

DUTCH. She's gotta go somewhere?

FLORENCE. To the little girl's room.

DUTCH. Oh.

FLORENCE. *(Tries to control her temper.)* She does this all the time. I told her she had to use the bed pan because I wasn't going to carry her after I got ready. *(To MOMMA.)* Momma I told you what we'd do, if this happened, didn't I?

MOMMA. I want to go down the hall.

FLORENCE. Jesus Christ, shit, Momma!

MOMMA. Shit, yourself!

DUTCH. Let's take a breath here. Let's not, y'know...

FLORENCE. Well, I'm not getting mussed up after all the work I had to do to look half way presentable.

MOMMA. It's not my fucking fault, is it?

DUTCH. I'll carry her, no problem, if that's okay. I can carry her. I mean, she's just going down the hall.

FLORENCE. She's being stubborn. *(Slow and emphatic.)* Dutch'll wait outside, Momma, while you use the pan, like they made me wait outside when you used it at the hospital.

MOMMA. I want to be carried!

DUTCH. I can do that. I can do that for her. I don't mind. Happy to help. Let's see what I can do. That OK with you Momma? You let me carry you down the hallway?

MOMMA. Better hurry up!

DUTCH. I'm gonna just lift you up and carry you Momma. No problem. I don't mind at all.

(He lifts MOMMA out of the lung. She's very small, frail.)

MOMMA. Wow! What big strong arms.
DUTCH. You're light as a feather.
FLORENCE. This way.
MOMMA. Hurry!
FLORENCE. We get her to the door, you can stand her up, and I can manage from there.
DUTCH. We're right behind you, right, Momma? Flying right behind you.

(They EXIT down the hall.)

FLORENCE. *(OFF)* OK. I got her. Hold on, Momma, take the wall. I got you.

(DUTCH ENTERS holding his shirt front out and looking at a
       wet spot.)

DUTCH. *(To himself, agitated.)* Hmmm. Well. I don't know. I guess it's...I don't know...urine.
FLORENCE. *(OFF)* Oh, God. Mama. Look what you did to yourself.
DUTCH. *(To himself.)* These things happen.

(He breathes to calm down.)

FLORENCE. *(OFF)* I told you to go before.
MOMMA. *(OFF)* Oh, fuck you.
FLORENCE. *(OFF)* Fuck you, Momma, and stay still.
DUTCH. *(To himself.)* These situations, helping someone.

FLORENCE. *(OFF)* Don't make me get mad!
DUTCH. *(To himself.)* Someone in this condition, I guess.
FLORENCE. *(OFF)* Stay still, goddamnit, Momma!
MOMMA. *(OFF)* Goddamnit, yourself!
DUTCH. *(To himself.)* These things happen. Just a human thing.
MOMMA. *(OFF)* You're not grateful! All I've done.
DUTCH. *(To himself.)* Human function. Something stops working.
MOMMA. All I've done for you.
DUTCH. *(To himself.)* Some body part. Some kind of gasket wears out. I don't know though. I don't know what to do now.
FLORENCE. *(OFF)* Dutch. You available? We need a good Samaritan here.
DUTCH. You bet.

(He EXITS to help.)

FLORENCE. *(OFF)* We had a false alarm, I think.
DUTCH. *(OFF)* OK, Momma, here we go.

(He ENTERS carrying MOMMA. She's in a different gown. He returns her to the lung.)

FLORENCE. Let's get you air.

(FLORENCE hooks MOMMA up to her oxygen. She puts MOMMA'S feet up on the pillow.)

MOMMA. I want my Tylenol. My back hurts!

FLORENCE. You're already had one. I'll give you one to-night.

MOMMA. I want it now.

FLORENCE. You have it now, I'm not giving you one tonight. The doctor said you could only have two a day and you've had one already.

MOMMA. I didn't have one.

FLORENCE. You did. If I give you one now, you won't get one tonight. You hear me?!

MOMMA. My back hurts so bad.

FLORENCE. You're back is fine! Dutch, you want another drink? Don't say nothing, Momma, I'm asking Dutch.

DUTCH. I had better pace myself, y'know, if I'm gonna drive us somewhere.

MOMMA. I want my Tylenol.

FLORENCE. I'm getting the fucking Tylenol!

(She EXITS. DUTCH fans his shirt front to dry it.)

DUTCH. *(To himself.)* Oh, boy. I don't know here. I got a problem. I got a little problem here.

MOMMA. Florence...!

(FLORENCE RETURNS with a Tylenol and a glass of water.)

FLORENCE. Stop yelling! She likes her extra strength Tylenol. The doctor cut her down to two a day because of her bladder.

MOMMA. What good is he? He never sees me.

(She gives MOMMA the pill and the water chaser.)

DUTCH. I was thinking, maybe, I should go to take care of a little problem that's come up. My shirt, for sure, got a little wet in the middle here.

FLORENCE. Oh, my God.

DUTCH. The pants are OK, I think, but the shirt isn't too good.

FLORENCE. Let me see. That's awful.

DUTCH. Don't say anything. Don't make her feel bad. It's just one of those human things that happens.

FLORENCE. I saw she had an accident but I thought it was after you left. That's why I said it was a false alarm because I didn't want to say anything.

DUTCH. Maybe I can just go.

FLORENCE. No. Don't make me feel worse. It was my Momma peed on you. Take it off and I'll wash it, and throw it in the dryer.

DUTCH. Well...

FLORENCE. We have time, come on, or I won't feel right.

DUTCH. OK.

(He takes off his shirt.)

FLORENCE. You might as well gimme the pants and let me see if they got spotted.

DUTCH. My pants?

FLORENCE. I'm not looking to see your equipment.

DUTCH. What?

FLORENCE. There's a big towel in the bathroom you can wrap around yourself, if you're shy.

DUTCH. Do it for me like a good boy and make me feel better.

(He EXITS. FLORENCE takes a drink.)

FLORENCE. There should be a big beach towel there with fish on it, I think.
DUTCH. *(OFF)* There's one with mermaids on it.
FLORENCE. It's a big one?
DUTCH. *(OFF)* Pretty big.
FLORENCE. That's it.

(Doorbell rings.)

DUTCH. *(OFF)* I appreciate you going through all this trouble.
FLORENCE. Someone's at the door. I'll be right back.

(FLORENCE EXITS.)
DUTCH. *(OFF)* I mean, if you think this is what should be done, I'm there!

(DUTCH ENTERS carrying his shirt and trousers, the mermaid towel wrapped around him, and finds the room empty, except for MOMMA, who snores a couple snores that quickly subside.)

DUTCH. *(To himself, quietly.)* Oh. Hmmm. I don't know. I don't know about this. *(Breathes to relax.)* You probably know best. I haven't met someone nice — let me say it — as nice and...and...

(FLORENCE ENTERS with MRS. STAMEN, a middle aged woman. She carries a book of religious writing, and a book of hymns.)

FLORENCE. Dutch this is Mrs. Stamen.
DUTCH. Hello.
FLORENCE. *(Getting the shirt and pants from DUTCH.)* Gimme those and I'll go throw them in. *(To MRS. STAMEN.)* There was a little accident helping Momma. *(To DUTCH.)* Mrs. Stamen's from Momma's church. They keep her company when they can. *(Crosses to MOMMA.)* Momma, Mrs. Stamen's here. Momma your friend from the church is here. *(Observes MOMMA a moment.)* Momma? *(Quietly)* She's asleep. *(To MRS. STAMEN.)* Sit down, Mrs. Stamen. There's a pot of coffee, I know you take decaf, and there's a sandwich in the fridge. Would you like something now?
MRS. STAMEN. Not now, thank you.
FLORENCE. I got you some of that good feta you like.
MRS. STAMEN. It was my husband liked feta.
FLORENCE. Yes, he did, didn't he? Well, I'll go down to the laundry room. I won't be long. You're all right?
DUTCH. Oh, yeah. Fine.
FLORENCE. *(To MRS. STAMEN.)* I'll close Momma up so she can breathe easier. She should sleep for a little while, than you can open her up, so you two can visit.

(She closes the top of the iron-lung-like affair that is MOMMA'S bed. The activated devise makes a steady breathing sound — and an intermittently louder "whoosh" that gets DUTCH'S attention, and makes him even more uneasy.

FLORENCE EXITS with the pants and shirt.)

MRS STAMEN. *(To DUTCH, after a moment.)* I don't like feta. Not really. But it was thoughtful.

DUTCH. *(Looking over at MOMMA'S breathing bed unit.)* Well, that's, ah, that's...

MRS. STAMEN. What?

DUTCH. What? Oh, I...

MRS. STAMEN. My husband liked feta. *(Smiles, chokes up.)* I would tease him. Call him Ol' Feta Breath.

DUTCH. Uh-huh.

MRS. STAMEN. I never liked it that much. But he always wanted it.

DUTCH. Is that right?

MRS. STAMEN. He passed away.

DUTCH. Oh, well, now I'm sorry to hear.

MRS. STAMEN. He loved his feta.

DUTCH. He did? I see.

MRS. STAMEN. What?

DUTCH. You say he loved feta. I understand.

MRS. STAMEN. Do you?

DUTCH. Yes. I understand when you love something.

MRS. STAMEN. He loved it, alright.

DUTCH. Yes.

MRS. STAMEN. He did.

DUTCH. I understand. But...um...tell me, because...what exactly is feta?

MRS. STAMEN. What is Feta?

DUTCH. Yes, I don't think I know exactly what that is.

MRS. STAMEN. You don't know what feta is?

DUTCH. Not exactly, no.

MRS. STAMEN. It's cheese, a feta cheese.

DUTCH. Oh, I like cheese, all kinds. Feta, though? I don't think...

MRS. STAMEN. It's Greek, and my husband was a Greek. I'm not but he was. He was born here, in this country, in Philadelphia, but he was Greek. I didn't know he was Greek until he told me, and I learned about the things he ate.

DUTCH. Well, now I know. You see, you meet someone, you can learn things.

MRS. STAMEN. It's made from sheep milk, sheep with goat milk sometimes, but it's made from sheep. He told me all about it. He learned about it from his mother, I guess, it was, though he didn't have too many good things to say about that woman. *(Pause)* Not much good at all. *(Pause)* He was a Christian, though. He loved Christ. I met him in church. A good man does loves Christ, and he loved Christ.

DUTCH. I'm definitely going to try that cheese. Feta cheese? *(Beat)* I work with an Italian, part Italian, his mother's Italian, and he's introduced me to all kinds of different Italian foods. And to a cheese called parmigiana.

MRS. STAMEN. *(Defensively)* My husband was Greek.

DUTCH. I know, I was just saying, I'm interested in trying some feta cheese someday, and all types of food really.

(DUTCH squirms uncomfortably. The rhythmical sound of the breathing apparatus — punctuated by an occasional "whoosh" — becomes more apparent in the silence between MRS STAMEN and DUTCH.)

MRS. STAMEN. Do you love Christ, our Saviour?

DUTCH. *(After a moment figuring out what she has asked.)* I do have personal beliefs.

MRS. STAMEN. Because if you don't believe in our Lord, Jesus Christ, and take him as your saviour, the road you travel will be so much harder.

DUTCH. Well...

MRS. STAMEN. It's the same road with or without Jesus, is my opinion, but it is so much harder without him.

DUTCH. Well, now, I appreciate what you're saying. Don't think I don't.

MRS. STAMEN. You know, a man lost in the desert, dying of thirst, met Jesus and he led him to water, a beautiful oasis. He thought he had imagined it until he saw the foot prints in the sand, because Jesus walked him, and he was saved.

DUTCH. I respect your opinion. You have a right, an inalienable right, to the religion of your choice.

MRS. STAMEN. I can tell you're confused.

DUTCH. What?

MRS. STAMEN. That you're confused. It's hard for you to know what it is that you want. Maybe we should pray together, there's a special prayer I know that God always hears.

DUTCH. Well...

MRS. STAMEN. It's hard for you 'cause there's confusion inside.

DUTCH. I know your from a church, but...

MRS. STAMEN. I'm bothered by how things could turn out for you because of your confusion.

DUTCH. I don't know what you mean. Exactly. I'm trying here but...

MRS. STAMEN. You're taking Florence out into temptation tonight.

DUTCH. If you're concerned for Florence, she's a nice girl. I have nothing but respect for her.

MRS. STAMEN. Things can go wrong out in temptation.

DUTCH. I believe in doing good. Being positive. Looking for the best in people.

MRS. STAMEN. What would be inside if you cracked open like an egg? What would we see, all good, or would there be bad in there, too?

DUTCH. I don't know what you'd see, but I see the good in people.

MRS. STAMEN. You think people want it to be good? You don't think they wait for horrible things to happen?

DUTCH. That don't sound like life to me, as I know it.

MRS. STAMEN. *(Emotion rising.)* You don't think people want to see evil happen to others? People are waiting, waiting for something bad to happen to others, and it's going to happen. We just don't know when. I didn't know with my husband. I turned around and he was gone. It could happen to you tonight. You never know.

DUTCH. We're going out to have some fun. Nothing evil in that, I can see, if that's what's bothering you. We work hard and we're going out to have a good time. I haven't known her very long but I like her. I respect her and I like her. There's nothing negative in my heart. Nothing. Nothing bad.

MRS. STAMEN. Watch your step. Watch every step you take. Life has plenty good. Plenty. I want to say the prayer for you. Give me your hand and don't be afraid. Give me your hand!

(He gives her his hand.)

MRS. STAMEN. "Oh, that You would bless me indeed, and enlarge my territory, that YOUR hand would be with me, and that You would keep me from evil, that I may not cause pain."

(They hold hands in silence.)

    DUTCH. Life has good more than bad.
    MRS. STAMEN. Ow...
    DUTCH. I see good.
    MRS. STAMEN. You're squeezing. My hand.

(DUTCH let's go.)

    DUTCH. I'm sorry.
    MRS. STAMEN. *(Angrily)* You should be more careful!
    DUTCH. I forget my strength. I'm sorry. My work, I'm always gripping the machine.
    MRS. STAMEN. *(Unpleasantly)* I'll bet you're going out to drinking and dancing, where things get set loose, set in motion, where sex and evil is in the air. It doesn't go in a straight line. It leaps around like an electrical current. And it will bite you like a serpent!

*(DUTCH is dumbfounded. In silence the breathing unit makes
    its soft "whooshing" sound.)*

    DUTCH. I'm gonna, if you'll excuse me, I'm gonna clean up some, so I'll just be back there if anyone needs me. I'll be in the bathroom washing up.

*(He starts out. MRS. STAMEN begins singing and he stops as
    she sings. He listens then backs out down the hall. MRS.*

*STAMEN sings in his direction, then moves and sings next
to MOMMA'S breathing unit.)*

MRS. STAMEN.
(Sings)
LITTLE LAMB, WHO MADE THEE?
DOST THOU KNOW WHO MADE THEE,
GAVE THEE LIFE, AND BADE THEE FEED
BY THE STREAM AND O'ER THE MEAD;
GAVE THEE CLOTHING OF DELIGHT,
SOFTEST CLOTHING, WOOLLY, BRIGHT;
GAVE THEE SUCH A TENDER VOICE,
MAKING ALL THE VALES REJOICE?
LITTLE LAMB, WHO MADE THEE?
DOST THOU KNOW WHO MADE THEE?

Scene 7

*(A bar. Jukebox stage left. FLORENCE, DUTCH, PHYLLIS
and MARTY at a booth. Drinks. MARTY is in his Saturday
night clothes. PHYLLIS has dressed up, too. MARTY lifts a
cherry by its stem from a rocks glass containing four cher-
ries. He moves it toward PHYLLIS.)*

MARTY. Here it comes. Nice red cherry. Nice and sweet.
Come on...

*(MARTY feeds PHYLLIS the cherry. She eats it, smiling and
laughing.)*

MARTY. Tell us how old you were.
PHYLLIS. A long time ago.
MARTY. You ate it. You got to tell us.

(They wait. MARTY grins at DUTCH, who is unsure how to take the game.)

PHYLLIS. Sixteen.
MARTY. Woooooie!
PHYLLIS. My cherry got drove so far back it became a tail light.

(FLORENCE and PHYLLIS have a big laugh. MARTY joins them. DUTCH is till unsure.)

MARTY. *(To DUTCH.)* See, a good ice-breaker!
FLORENCE. One of you next.
MARTY. Ladies choice.

(FLORENCE takes the cherry and moves it toward DUTCH.)

FLORENCE. Dutch?

(DUTCH stares at the cherry.)

DUTCH. Well...

(He draws back from it.)

PHYLLIS. Drink up, so you'll loosen up.
DUTCH. No, I think I'm starting to feel it. I don't know,

maybe it's going a little fast here.

FLORENCE. We're all getting loose. I have a little buzz. You feeling it Phyllis?

PHYLLIS. I feel good. Yeah. Time to rip it up.

MARTY. Oh-oh. We're in danger, Dutch.

FLORENCE. Eat your cherry.

MARTY. Come on, you don't want to get left behind. Knock down some courage.

(DUTCH tosses down a shot of tequila. FLORENCE holds the cherry in front of DUTCH, who stares at it closed mouth, after a moment, she moves the cherry to her own mouth.)

FLORENCE. I was eighteen.

(She opens her mouth and lowers the cherry into it.)

FLORENCE. Mmmm. He thought he talked me into it, but I had to just get it over. It was all I could think about.

MARTY. See what we're learning? All right, all right. I'll go next. We're talking about my cherry now. *(Chews)* Thirteen.

PHYLLIS. All guys say thirteen.

MARTY. Thirteen. I swear to God. My second cousin. Training to be a nurse. Dutch knows.

(FLORENCE takes up the last cherry and moves it toward DUTCH. They focus their attention on him.)

FLORENCE. Open up.

(He eats it. Pause.)

DUTCH. Well, I...
FLORENCE. He's blushing...Oh.

(She gives him a kiss on the cheek.)

MARTY. *(Pinches his cheeks.)* I'm blushing, too.

(He leans in for a kiss. She kisses him on the cheek.)

MARTY. *(To PHYLLIS.)* You're looking a little red, there.

(He kisses her on the cheek.)

FLORENCE. You owe one to Dutch, now, Phyllis. Phyllis gives Dutch a kiss on the cheek.
MARTY. My man! So how old were you??
DUTCH. *(Struggles)* Ah...Well...
PHYLLIS. I'm gonna guess. Thirteen.
DUTCH. No...
FLORENCE. Between thirteen to sixteen?
DUTCH. Well...
PHYLLIS. Sixteen to twenty one?
DUTCH. No...
FLORENCE. Twenty to thirty?
MARTY. It don't work to play the virgin. I tried it once and got flushed straight down the toilet.
FLORENCE. That'd be a miracle nowadays, a man saving himself.
PHYLLIS. They'd make a movie about it.

DUTCH. I don't feel comfortable, that's all, talking about it.

FLORENCE. We're all lying anyway.

PHYLLIS. Yeah.

FLORENCE. Oh, God, wait — under twelve? *(Expecting to be impressed.)* Dutch, was it under twelve?

DUTCH. No, no.

MARTY. Look, you don't want to talk about it?

DUTCH. Maybe, not.

MARTY. Well, OK. Let's move it along. A toast to the ladies. It's a pleasure to meet you both.

FLORENCE. *(To PHYLLIS.)* That's nice to hear said for a change, isn't it?

PHYLLIS. A pretty good first impression.

(FLORENCE moves to the music.)

FLORENCE. I like this music. You like it, Phyllis?

PHYLLIS. Yeah.

FLORENCE. Makes me move. You think you want to dance, Dutch?

DUTCH. Maybe a slow one, if it plays.

PHYLLIS. *(To FLORENCE; re: music.)* It kind of gets to you, huh?

(The two women move in rhythm to the music.)

FLORENCE. How about it, Marty, you gonna dance with Phyllis?

MARTY. I'm gonna warm up, and then look out.

FLORENCE. Come on Phyllis. Let's don't waste this

sitting down. *(As she gets up to dance, to DUTCH.)* Go play something slow, then, so I can get you started.

(FLORENCE and PHYLLIS dance. FLORENCE looks over at the men. Does a little sexy move for their benefit. MARTY gets up, and indicates a dance move for the ladies on his way to the jukebox.)

MARTY. Dutch!

(DUTCH follows MARTY to the jukebox.)

MARTY. Maybe you can work it out so you can bring her over.

DUTCH. I don't think so.

MARTY. We can go to my place. The other one will wanna go, I think, definitely.

DUTCH. She's got her mother and this woman watching her while she's out for awhile, so, you know.

MARTY. You want me to ask her, though?

DUTCH. You're gonna ask her?

MARTY. If she wants to come over with you.

DUTCH. She has her mother and it'll be late.

MARTY. It's her mother's the problem?

DUTCH. She's blind and has trouble breathing.

MARTY. If she says she can come, you wanna come or not?

DUTCH. If she says so, but I don't know, though, her mother, y'know, depends on her.

MARTY. Listen to Marty. Get with the program. Nothing to be confused about, I'm telling you. We play it right, you're gonna get everything you want.

DUTCH. I'm getting to know her better. You know, getting acquainted.

MARTY. She's practically asking to get laid, both of them.

DUTCH. What?

MARTY. I'm gonna ask her to dance, that OK with you, if I slow dance with her, so I can see if she'll come?

DUTCH. Well, yeah, sure, Marty.

MARTY. Then I can see if she can come over. You should ask the other one to dance.

DUTCH. Phyllis?

MARTY. Yeah, Phyllis, it's only polite. When I dance with yours, you ask mine. You want to get the drinks this time?

DUTCH. You think we're gonna want more?

MARTY. Another round, yeah, so things stay loosened up. (*Downs his drink.*) Pick something slow you like. (*Moving away.*) I think I got the rhythm. (*Dances toward the women.*) I got the rhythm. (*Joins the women.*) Oh, yeah. Look at these ladies.

(*MARTY and the women dance. DUTCH watches.*)

FLORENCE. (*Loudly*) We're missing someone.
PHYLLIS. Come on, Dutch!
MARTY. We got it going here!

(*DUTCH signals he's getting drinks. EXITS. MARTY, PHYL-LIS, FLORENCE dance. DUTCH RETURNS with drinks. He watches. Dance ends. Slow song plays. FLORENCE leads DUTCH to the floor. An awkwardness on his part.*)

FLORENCE. I like your friend. You're right, he knows how to have a good time.

DUTCH. Marty's good at having fun.

FLORENCE. I know I have to let loose once a week or I go out of my mind.

DUTCH. I get up pretty early, so it stops me from enjoying myself too much at night.

FLORENCE. You don't let off a little steam you pop. *(Moves closer.)* Let's try a turn. Come on. Just make a circle.

DUTCH. OK.

(They turn.)

FLORENCE. Good, Dutch. That's it. Good.

(DUTCH stops slow dancing.)

DUTCH. My boss, Pete, would have women over. He wasn't married then. So one time, he invited me, and he had this woman come over. And then he sent me down the hall to the bedroom, and she was in there.

FLORENCE. Yeah?

DUTCH. I was twenty-four.

FLORENCE. Oh...OK...

DUTCH. I didn't know her. I think you should. I think it should be special. You should care for one another. Get to know each other. I've thought about it, and the woman was probably a prostitute, and that's not the same.

(FLORENCE doesn't know what to make of it. They resume

*dancing. MARTY and PHYLLIS move into the light. He
holds her in a close, suave, slow dance position.)*

MARTY. Oh, no, no. No, listen, I don't live at my mom's.
I stay there part of the time because she's alone, and she likes a
man to be around the place. She cooks and cleans and does the
laundry. She loves to do it. I mention getting help, she throws
a fit. It's a big place. She goes to bed early. Nothing wakes her.
It's like my place, like my own place, though, you know? I do
what I want.

PHYLLIS. Uh-huh. She likes you around part of the time.
Sounds OK.

MARTY. I thought we'd go tonight. She made a beautiful
sausage 'n' marinara. I'm wondering, though, if you eat meat
because I know so many people don't.

PHYLLIS. Meat, sure. I eat it.

MARTY. Because there's some beautiful calamari if you
don't, and also, a beautiful vegetable antipasti, some beautiful,
beautiful food. You eat meat though?

PHYLLIS. You should see me tear into a plate of Flo's
ribs.

MARTY. So you want to come over?

PHYLLIS. To your mom's?

MARTY. It's more my place, y'know. I pay for everything.
We can get to know each other.

PHYLLIS. If your mom's there, I don't know.

MARTY. You won't even know she's there.

PHYLLIS. I don't know.

MARTY. I've got a beautiful bottle of Italian wine, a beautiful chianti. And a bottle of French champagne, a beautiful bottle
of Dom Perignon to have with the chocolate cake, a beautiful
cake. I guarantee satisfaction. You like to be satisfied?

PHYLLIS. Yeah, sure I do, but, y'know, satisfied means something to a Night Stalker it don't mean to me.

MARTY. You know what we have in common? I mean, I love your sense of humor, but you know something else I really love? You've got a strong physical feel about you.

PHYLLIS. A sixty foot truck holds a lot of cases to move in and out.

MARTY. I love that you're strong. I like holding you. I can feel the power. Like two animals dancing, like a bull and a horse. Usually I go for a woman has a more feminine... a shapeliness...but, I mean, don't get me wrong. There's a charge I get with you, an electric thing totally surprises me, so I'm gonna keep trying, I mean, if you don't say shut up, leave me alone, I figure, y'know, I got a shot.

PHYLLIS. I don't know what to say.

MARTY. Beautiful food, and the beautiful French champagne.

PHYLLIS. I don't think Florence can come. She has her mom at home needs care. Maybe she can.

MARTY. Well, we'll see, OK? You never know 'till you ask. I'll have a dance with her. See if she can. I know I want you there, though. *(He pulls her tight and they turn. DUTCH and FLORENCE move into view. They switch partners. MARTY pulls FLORENCE a little tighter as they move more prominently into the light, one arm around her waist, the other in a formal. As they slow dance.)* You guys have something going? You and Dutch? The chemistry is good?

FLORENCE. He's a good guy. I don't meet that many. The original Good Samaritan.

MARTY. It's good you're with him and not me then, because I'm not good. I love you all too much. Everyone of you.

Especially I see someone like you. Someone's got a special motion. Someone soft, looks like you, and is a pleasure to hold, like a beautiful cloud of flesh in my arms. I float right away. Float, float, away to heaven.

(They dance to the rear and eventually out of sight. DUTCH and PHYLLIS dance into the light. She is bored.)

DUTCH. I'll do a bathroom, for instance, and I'll think when I'm working, if people realize it, all the work goes into it, and not just about what I do, and I'll think of all the people that'll come in to use this bathroom, do they even know all the work? The carpenters and the insulation, the electrical, and, of course, the plumbing, and the painters. How many even think about it? How many even notice? All the hours of work?

PHYLLIS. *(Trying to sound interested.)* Yeah. Well, I go in, I won't pee the same, I guess.

DUTCH. *(Looks around.)* She must've found that cigarette. I didn't know she smoked. Her mother don't breathe too good, though.

(The lights fade on DUTCH and PHYLLIS. They come up on MARTY and FLORENCE outside the bar. FLORENCE smoking. She takes a deep drag. Let's the smoke out sensually.)

FLORENCE. I don't smoke much, but I love it when I have one.

MARTY. I saw you and I thought there's a woman isn't afraid to be a woman and enjoy things.

FLORENCE. I'm taking that as a compliment.

MARTY. That's why I'd hoped you'd come over.

FLORENCE. I can't tonight.

MARTY. Maybe some other time.

FLORENCE. Yeah?

MARTY. Maybe some other time you come over and I'll serve you dinner.

FLORENCE. What about your friend? Maybe he won't like you asking me.

MARTY. He don't need to know.

FLORENCE. You're a devil.

MARTY. No, I'm a tile setter. They pulled me to work with Dutch because they're behind. I'm really a tile setter, a journeyman.

FLORENCE. I'll bet the devil can set tile.

MARTY. You've seen the blue domes up on the cathedral where we're working?

FLORENCE. Up on the hill.

MARTY. I set the tile up there. Blue mosaic domes with ribs of gold tile dividing the sections.

FLORENCE. Real gold?

MARTY. Real gold mica, so it sparkles when the sun hits it. You should see them up close. You see how big the domes are up on top. You come up there you can see the fleurs de lis. A beautiful mosaic of white and yellow lilies I put in piece by piece on each dome. Cut and fit 'em, so they're spaced perfectly. Grout them, wash 'em clean. You can really appreciate them up close. We could go up there and have the whole roof to ourselves, have some wine and look at the view. You can see the mountains. You can see all the way to the ocean. I'm gonna want to put my hands on you. I can imagine what it must be like to show that you have some tenderness. Something I'd like to do now, if I could. You're so wonderful to look at, so good to imagine, to reach out and feel your breasts, get a feel of the weight soft in my hands. That'd be a dream to me. I want you to know that's what I'll be wanting to do if I get you up there on top the cathedral to see the domes.

(They stand motionless a moment. His hand cupping her breast.)

FLORENCE. *(Puts out her smoke; smiles.)* Devil, devil, devil.

(She starts back into the bar. DUTCH comes out.)

FLORENCE. One for the road and then I should think about getting back.
DUTCH. OK.
FLORENCE. I'll just make a trip to the ladies room first.

(FLORENCE EXITS into the bar.)

MARTY. You're right. It's her mother. Not you. She likes you. *(Pause)* She ain't bad. *(Beat)* We was talking about you. All your good points. I get the impression, don't take it wrong, like I say, she ain't bad, and she likes you, but I get the impression she plays the field a little. Nothing wrong with that, I don't think.
DUTCH. No, I know.
MARTY. It's an impression.
DUTCH. Well, a single woman.
MARTY. That's what I'm saying. *(Puts an arm on DUTCH'S*

shoulder.) Time to give Phyllis my full attention. She's ready I believe. I do believe she's ready for the take down.

(MARTY EXITS into the bar. DUTCH struggles silently with his thoughts.)

DUTCH. *(Talks to himself.)* What does he know. What? What does he know about it? *(Pause)* I'd rather, though, all the same, you didn't talk to her so long, or, at all, maybe — not at all.

(Lights fade on DUTCH and come up on PHYLLIS and FLOR-ENCE in a stall in the ladies room of the bar. FLORENCE is seated. Laughter.)

FLORENCE. I couldn't believe he said it.
PHYLLIS. He said it, though?
FLORENCE. Yes, he said it. You tell me if he's any good, then I might try him out.
PHYLLIS. He'll probably eat me up like a pizza pie!

(FLORENCE realizes there's no toilet paper.)

FLORENCE. This always happens.
PHYLLIS. What?
FLORENCE. There's no toilet paper.
PHYLLIS. I'll get you something.

(PHYLLIS EXITS the stall and the ladies room. FLORENCE sits resignedly waiting.)

FLORENCE. *(As though talking to PHYLLIS.)* I wish I could go over there. I worry about Mama, though, choking to death, or something. Sometimes I want to cut loose and not care. That'd be something. We went over there and went crazy all night. There's Mama, though, so I can never do anything like it, really. I work and take care of her and sneak out like this once a month if I'm lucky. Sometimes I wish she'd just go. I wish she'd go and I could live more. I'm terrible to think that, ain't I? I can't help it, though. *(Pause)* Phyllis? Phyllis? You get lost? *(Beat)* Phyllis!

(Light fades.)

Scene 8

(MARTY stands dressed for work. MARTY'S MOM moves in and out of light.)

MOM. You sounded like animals running loose.

MARTY. Someone from work came over. We were fooling around, having a little fun, rough housing a little.

MOM. Rough housing?

MARTY. We arm wrestled. I'm sorry I woke you.

MOM. I thought it was an earthquake.

MARTY. A buddy from work.

MOM. I want him to pay for the fucking dishes he broke. What kind of asshole is he anyway? I don't want you bringing people like that over. You hear me? All the cooking I do. All the cleaning. The washing. You thank me by bringing someone over that breaks things!

MARTY. What do you want me to do Mom, slit my fucking throat? I said I'm sorry.

MOM. Slit it. Go ahead. Slit your throat and leave me alone! Serve me right for giving birth! Two days I was in labor! Shoulders two feet wide! I died for you! The thanks I get is you bring drunks over to eat everything and break up my house! You know the rules. You don't like the rules move out. You're what, thirty fucking-five years old! You can move out and see what it's like to keep a place! See what it's like to cook and do the cleaning!

MARTY. How many times I said I'll hire someone to help? How many times?

MOM. I made your fucking lunch, though you don't deserve it. So don't say goodbye and don't fucking thank me!

(Sound of door slamming shut. He walks upstage and shouts off to his mom.)

MARTY. Jesus, shit, mom, come on. I fucking said I'm sorry.

MOM. *(OFF)* Watch your mouth!

MARTY. You know I love the lunch. You know that. I love it. I'm not going till you say goodbye. Mom? I'm not going. You hear? I'll fucking be late for work but I'm not going until you say goodbye. Mom? Goodbye. I'm saying goodbye. *(Screams)* I'm saying fucking goodbye!

Scene 9

*(Construction site. BANANAS crosses above on scaffold with
hod. DUTCH slowly moves across stage with a floor grinder, power cable wrapped around his shoulder. MARTY
scoops pucciorino with a wide shovel and dumps it into a
wheel barrow.)*

MARTY. Too bad you couldn't come over. Unbelievable.
We ate. We drank all the wine. I took a big handful of the chocolate cake and fed it to her. Next thing we're naked. I spread her
out on the table. I was a fucking animal I saw her like that. That
black meadowland, that open pink melon. My fucking cock was
hard as fucking rock. I fucked her in the kitchen on the table.
She was spread out there, the left over calamari and veal, and
she spread her legs up, and I went fucking wild, fucking plates
of food all around like a feast. You would've come over, who
knows, you know?

*(He wheels the slop out. DUTCH keeps moving the machine
evenly across the floor. Eventually sounds of construction
stop — as day turns to night — except for the sound of
DUTCH'S machine. DUTCH, alone, working under drop
lights, moves slowly up and down with the floor grinder.
Sound of machine gives way to sound of assisted breathing.)*

Scene 10

*(FLORENCE'S apartment. FLORENCE stands by the iron
      lung.)*

FLORENCE. It has big blue domes on top, you can see
'em up on the hill, blue mosaic tile domes, with gold ribs that
divide it, and a design of a big flower, he said, was called a
fleurs de lis. He said it was real gold mica flakes in it. You can
see 'em sparkle. He wants to show off the work he did to me.
He said you can see the whole city, all the way to the ocean. I've
got two men after me that work together. You had that problem with Daddy and his friend, and I was wondering how you
handled it, because they never found out for a long time. Dutch
is dependable, I think, and a good man. Marty thinks he's a hot
shot, thinks he's a wolf. Bad like Daddy's friend was. I'm hop-
ing you'll say something might help without giving me some
smartass remark. Momma? *(Moves closer to lung.)* Momma?
(Pause) Oh, Momma, no...

*(She stands looking down into the lung. Lighting changes to
      isolate FLORENCE and reveal DUTCH standing at work
      site, shirt off, a sqeegee and work rags in his hands. He
      looks off in the direction of FLORENCE.)*

DUTCH. I want to say what I think to you. I want to have
the words. I want to be able to let you know how I feel. I want
to say what you like to hear. I want to make you laugh. I want
to tell you I love you. I want you to be happy. I want to work
overtime and give you my paycheck. I want you to feel safe. I
want you to have a good time. I want you never to have to work.

I want to worship you. I want you to feel like a goddess. I want to buy you a dress. I want to make your heart beat fast. I want to say the right things. I want to touch you in the right places. I want to know what to do. I want to drive you crazy. I want to not let you go. I want to be an animal when you want. Take you by force when you want. Not move when you want. Take orders when you want. I want you to toss and turn when I'm not there. I want to talk dirty in your ear. I want to talk like the devil. I want to howl like a dog.

(Lights fade out.)

Scene 11

(Construction site. Sound of nail guns firing in patterns. Impression of stained glass windows catching light in rear. DUTCH and MARTY are on their hands and knees, shirts off, sealing the floor with rags in wide broad strokes.)

MARTY. Like I say, she said she wanted to see them so I thought I'd show her, unless you say no, y'know, don't for some reason. No big deal. It's not like you're going out now, right?
DUTCH. What?
MARTY. If you were going together or something. Seeing each other, y'know, something serious or something.
DUTCH. What?
MARTY. It'd be different.

(DUTCH stares blankly.)

DUTCH. Uh-huh. *(Beat)* This green came out pretty good with the rose and the raw sienna.

MARTY. *(Without enthusiasm.)* Looks good.

DUTCH. Makes it worthwhile.

MARTY. Huh?

DUTCH. All the work. When you see it, y'know, when it's done.

MARTY. So, have you talked to her lately?

DUTCH. Not since her mom died.

MARTY. Her mom died?

DUTCH. She didn't say much.

MARTY. She was OK, though?

DUTCH. They were close, I guess.

MARTY. You didn't say anything that she died.

DUTCH. I didn't know what to say to her.

MARTY. You didn't mention her mom.

DUTCH. She said she needed some time, but if you're gonna show her, she wants to go, well...y'know...

(They've finished wiping down the sealer. They gather sealer can and put rags in a five gallon bucket.)

MARTY. So when was this, with her mom?

DUTCH. Couple weeks.

MARTY. Maybe it's a good time I ask her, then, y'know, so she gets out. A friendly type thing. I can imagine if it was my mom. You weren't close to your mom, so...maybe that's why you didn't know what to say. But I can imagine if it was mine.

DUTCH. I said I felt bad.

MARTY. So I'm gonna ask her, since you're not seeing her now.

DUTCH. She wants to go, that's for her to decide.

MARTY. She wants to, that's what I'm saying. Maybe Sunday.

DUTCH. You asked her?

MARTY. She said she'd like to see them up close, so, maybe Sunday.

DUTCH. Well, so you're gonna take her?

MARTY. Like I say, you're not seeing her, right?

DUTCH. I know.

MARTY. So everything's OK?

DUTCH. I guess. Sure.

MARTY. Everything's OK between us?

(They walk from the finished floor to the exterior of he site.)

DUTCH. Yeah, Marty...The electrician's done in the small bathroom so I'm gonna do the fine grind and seal it before I go.

MARTY. I'm taking off then. You're staying, I'll see ya Monday.

DUTCH. Yeah. We'll be in the other building.

MARTY. OK. *(Puts an arm around DUTCH'S shoulder.)* Listen to Marty now, you hear, and don't fucking work all night. You hear me?

DUTCH. No, no.

MARTY. OK? I want you to listen. Do something Sunday. Have some fun.

(DUTCH puts his arms around MARTY in a swift tight, hug.)

DUTCH. Sure. And you do what you do Sunday. You do what you do.

(DUTCH tightens harder.)

MARTY. You gone queer on me? All right. Let me the fuck go.

(MARTY has trouble breathing. Paralyzed by DUTCH'S grip.)

DUTCH. You worried about me? Worried I work too much?

(MARTY struggles, his arms trapped, gasping.)

MARTY. Fucking prick!
DUTCH. I hear you. I'm listening...I'm listening to you, Marty.

(DUTCH lets MARTY go. MARTY staggers a bit, furious.)

MARTY. Idiot. Idiot fucking moron! Now I'm gonna fuck her. I'm gonna fuck her for you. I'm gonna fuck her and your gonna be here eating fucking pucciorino! I'll be eating pussy. *(He gets into DUTCH'S face.)*

MARTY. Idiot grinder, that's what you are, that's all you are, an idiot fucking terrazzo grinder.

(DUTCH grabs MARTY again in a powerful bear hug.)

DUTCH. You didn't get enough? Huh, Marty? You didn't get enough?

*(MARTY tries to struggle, makes violent animal sounds of pro-
test, DUTCH crushes him to silence, lifting him off the
ground in the process.)*

DUTCH. *(Outburst)* Maybe you shouldn't ask her anything. So don't. Maybe that's how it is, too. Don't ask her and
don't take her anywhere.

*(He lets him fall to the ground. DUTCH, emotionally detached,
looks on as MARTY twitches spasmodically a moment,
then stops. After a pause, as though routine, DUTCH picks
up a five gallon work bucket, bangs it clean of any debris,
and puts it in the tool box. He drags MARTY to the tool
box and puts him in it. He picks up a couple other tools,
and puts them in the box, too. He shuts the lid. DUTCH
stands a moment, as though disconnected to the violence
that has happened, then he opens the lid and looks in at
MARTY'S lifeless body. He pulls MARTY'S body up by the
shirt, shakes it.)*

DUTCH. Marty?

*(He lets the body fall back in. He closes the lid, latches and
locks it shut. Stands motionless a moment before he gathers
and pulls on his yellow slicker top, puts on his gloves.)*

DUTCH. I can't control what they say. What they say or
what they do. That's the way it is. I can't control what I think,
can I? I wanted to hit him in the head with the hammer and fuck
up the floor with his blood and brains. I didn't do it, but I can't
control that I thought it, that I saw it. That's the way it is.

(He puts his air filter mask on. Picks up the hand grinder and walks deeper into the building and begins fine grinding the wall of a small room. The white cement and marble dust begins to cloud the room.

Day turns to night. A work light illuminates the dust-filled room as DUTCH grinds.

Day breaks and grows lighter. Muted sound of construction from inside the site. DUTCH works on, a ghost image in the fine marble dust, moving his machine in slow circles as he polish grinds the wall.

Construction sound grows louder. BANANAS crosses the scaffold, a heavy hod of wet plaster on his shoulder, and EXITS from sight.

Fade out.)

THE END